C000157533

THE LITTLE BOOK OF

ENGLAND FOOTBALL

EDITED BY IAIN SPRAGG

This edition published in 2020 by OH!
part of Welbeck Publishing Group
20 Mortimer Street, London, W1T 3JW

A CIP catalogue record of this book is available from the British Library.

ISBN 978 1 78739 344 8

Printed in Dubai

10 9 8 7 6 5 4 3 2 1

Contents

INTRODUCTION

Dedicated to the wit and wisdom of famous present and former England players and managers, as well as those who've come face-to-face with the feared Three Lions, *The Little Book of England Football* is a must-read for every fan of the beautiful game's oldest international team.

Featuring quotes from some of the team's greatest ever players such as Sir Bobby Charlton, David Beckham and Harry Kane, plus the thoughts of legendary managers Sir Alf Ramsey, Sir Bobby Robson and Gareth Southgate, the book encapsulates everything that makes England the most iconic side in world football.

Chapters include a celebration of the Three Lions' rollercoaster World Cup exploits, the team's fiercest and occasionally most bad-tempered international rivalries and the thoughts of those fortunate enough to have played at Wembley, the home of football. There's also a chapter full of quotes from England's army of celebrity supporters.

England played in the first ever football international back in 1872, and *The Little Book of England Football* is all about celebrating the famous white (and occasionally red, blue and grey) shirt and the players who have worn it with pride for almost one and a half centuries.

CHAPTER 1

WE LOVE YOU ENGLAND, WE DO

"If I had to die on a football pitch,
I would want to do it playing for England.
You should be willing to lay down your life
and I wouldn't forgive any player who didn't
give it their all. Playing for your country
is the greatest honour.**"**

IAN WRIGHT

bristling with pride

"Playing for your country is a magical moment and for me it was the start of everything I dreamed of achieving in my senior career.**"**

HARRY KANE

England's captain at the 2018 World Cup

❝Representing your country is the ultimate honour. A player takes pride in his shirt every step of the way but nothing compares with the feeling when you walk out for the first time in your country's colours.**❞**

BRYAN ROBSON

who debuted against the Republic of Ireland in February 1980

"England can end the Millennium as it started – as the greatest football nation in the world.**"**

KEVIN KEEGAN

the eternal optimist in 1999 (and historically inaccurate)

❝It's indescribable really. You just get that adrenalin rush through your body. But you just know once you've got that shirt on and once you're on the pitch, then that's when you're at home and that's when you want to perform and do your best.**❞**

DANNY WELBECK

on playing for England

"As a kid I always loved watching
a big England game on the television.
Back then I had a burning ambition to play
for my country. To be appointed captain
is beyond my wildest dreams.**"**

WAYNE ROONEY

on wearing the captain's armband for the first time, 2009

❝No money in the world can buy a white England shirt.**❞**

ALAN SHEARER

whose seven goals ranks third all-time in European Championships

❝I love playing for England. I've been in 60 or 70 squads now and I still appreciate I'm being picked as one of the best players in the country. To ever think that playing for England is a bit of a burden is something I'd never say.**❞**

RIO FERDINAND

doesn't feel the pressure

❝You look around and think 'I remember watching them on the telly – they're England.' And you don't feel as if you should be here with them.**❞**

CHRIS WADDLE

England midfielder in the 1980s and 90s

""Scoring two goals at Wembley against a Dutch team that was supposed to rip us apart and ripping them apart – it doesn't get better than that.**""**

TEDDY SHERINGHAM

who starred in England's 4–1 Euro 96 victory

"I love playing for my country. I see it as the biggest privilege of my career, so there's no way I'm going to volunteer to give that up. I want to on for as long as I can.**"**

JOHN TERRY

resists retirement

" Making my England debut was a
dream I had for 20 years. As soon as
I started to kick a ball, or was aware of it,
my one thing was to play for England. **"**

GARETH SOUTHGATE

England player at the 1998 World Cup and coach 20 years later

"Playing for England has got to be the best feeling in the world. It's the pinnacle. You can't really go any higher in the game than playing for your country. To put the shirt on and earn my first England cap was unbelievable.**"**

JORDAN PICKFORD

reflects on his international bow against Germany in 2017

"" Just getting picked for England was an honour and pulling on the number six jersey was incredible. How can you turn down the chance to play for your country? **""**

NORMAN HUNTER

defender who represented the Three Lions 28 times 1965–74

"Catch me if you can
Cos I'm the England man
And what you're looking at
Is the masterplan.**"**

JOHN BARNES

rapping on New Order's 'World in Motion' England's record for the
1990 World Cup

❝I have enjoyed every minute of representing my country and it is a sad day for me knowing that I won't pull on the England shirt again. This is one of the toughest decisions I've ever made.**❞**

STEVEN GERRARD

announces his international retirement, 2014

“I loved playing for England,
I love my country.**”**

GARY NEVILLE

who played in five major tournaments for the Three Lions

❝Managing England in Euro 96 and representing my country provided the best moments of my life, which I will never forget. It still gives me the goose pimples when you realise how much you can give back to your country.❞

TERRY VENABLES

the first man to play for England at every age group

"I loved playing for England, I loved every single game and they were the best experiences of my life.**"**

PAUL GASCOIGNE

outstanding midfielder and star of the 1990 World Cup

❝I got to be around an England team at a World Cup in Brazil, and that was an amazing experience.❞

ALEX OXLADE-CHAMBERLAIN

in England's 2014 squad aged 20

"I just want to make the nation proud of the England team, make people feel hope, bring back that happiness that comes with English football.**"**

JOHN STONES

defensive star at the 2018 World Cup

❝I was just a skinny kid from Nottingham making my debut for England. I never really thought about being the first black player. I never realised what a big deal it was until years afterwards. All I could think about was that I was playing alongside some great names.**❞**

VIV ANDERSON

on his historic international bow in 1978 against Czechoslovakia

❝Representing England was the ultimate honour for me. It meant so much to my family and the wider community.**❞**

ANDY COLE

15 caps and one goal for his country under four different managers

" To have the chance to do something for your nation I think blows everything out of the water. To represent your country, there's nothing better. **"**

KYLE WALKER

defender who won almost 50 caps in the 2010s

31

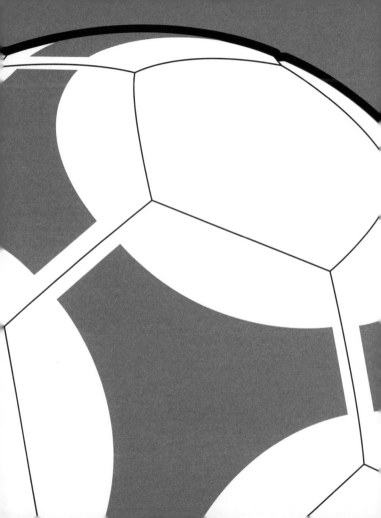

CHAPTER 2

HEROES OF THE SHIRT

"One of the reasons why I've never
retired from England is because if
there's ever an opportunity to play
for them again, then I'm available.**"**

DAVID BECKHAM

winner of 115 caps

"An England shirt carries a heavy load of responsibility. But it's a weight that England can place on my shoulders any time they like. It's a great honour, a marvellous experience and a wonderful thrill. If you ever get the chance, don't turn it down.**"**

EMLYN HUGHES

whose 62-cap Three Lions career spanned three decades

"People think you must be crackers if you've got a psychologist, but psychology is part of the building bricks to make a top athlete.**"**

DAVID JAMES

winner of 53 caps for his country between 1997 and 2010

" The mental strength, you've just got to have that because you get a lot of stick as a goalkeeper – you're the last line of defence. When a goal goes in everyone looks at you, you've got to be able to deal with that. If you make a mistake, it could be a bad mistake, how are you going to recover? Are you going to react positively or are you just going to cave in? **"**

DAVID SEAMAN

on the perils of life between the sticks

"Playing international football is something I always wanted to do as a young boy and I'm sure there's thousands and thousands of kids who dream and wake up every morning thinking that's what they want to be. I feel very proud and very privileged.**"**

HARRY MAGUIRE

a fan in the stands at EURO 2016 and star on the pitch at Russia 2018

"When I am playing for England, particularly abroad, I am conscious of the fact that I am representing everybody back home.**"**

ALAN BALL

1966 World Cup winner

"You come up against challenges in life, and it's how you deal with them that defines you.**"**

HARRY KANE

on dealing with expectations in 2015

"Playing for England was one long roller-coaster, some ups and downs, but also quite a few moments when you're not really sure if you're enjoying the ride.**"**

GARY NEVILLE

winner of 85 caps for his country

"Nothing is given to you. You've got to work for it."

JACK CHARLTON

Sir Bobby's big brother and 1966 World Cup winner

❝I want more from David Beckham.
I want him to improve on perfection.**❞**

KEVIN KEEGAN

England manager February 1999 to October 2000

"Even now after many appearances for England, I still get a great thrill at being selected, as I shall always.**"**

ALAN MULLERY

England midfielder between 1964 and 1971

" Even now kids come up to me and say, 'You're the one who won the World Cup and did that jig with no teeth'. **"**

NOBBY STILES

still being reminded of his glory 37 years later

❝I don't know why, but playing for England, I always feel I am going to score.**❞**

PETER CROUCH

who netted 22 times in 44 international appearances

❝I think self-belief is a massive thing in football. If you don't believe in yourself, not many others will. Work hard and believe in yourself, and I think you'll go as far as your body will take you.**❞**

HARRY KANE

The England captain's work ethic has paid dividends for club and country

❝I had the credibility, performance-wise, to be captain. I was consistently in the heart of the defence and I was a club captain early on in my career.**❞**

SOL CAMPBELL

laments never being named skipper during his 73-cap career

" If you never concede a goal, you're going to win more games than you lose. **"**

BOBBY MOORE

a big fan of clean sheets

❝I think about all my successes and failures, and sometimes the failures stick in your head as much as the wins. But you do move on.**❞**

FRANK LAMPARD

never stood still on England duty

" International football is about individual pride and wanting to perform at the highest level. If I got picked at 41, I would have played, even if I thought I would make a fool of myself. I just wanted to play for my country. **"**

SIR TREVOR BROOKING

was 33 when he won his last cap at the 1982 World Cup

" They've been brilliant ambassadors for our country, everybody can see they are proud to wear the shirt. **"**

GARETH SOUTHGATE

on his 2018 World Cup squad

"It's not just what you do on the pitch, it's what you do off the pitch.**"**

PAUL INCE

on why practice makes perfect

" Michael Owen is a goalscorer – not a natural born one, not yet, that takes time. **"**

GLENN HODDLE

England manager during the 1966 World Cup but, in Michael's case, it didn't take long.

❝Before games, people ask whether I get nervous. To be honest, I don't get nervous, I just enjoy it. I am living the dream. When I was a kid I always wanted to play for my country and now I am here, I will enjoy it.**❞**

JERMAIN DEFOE

scorer of 20 goals in 57 games for the Three Lions

" Good luck to the team out there, the players know that even though I won't be there, I will have my England shirt on as a fan this time and supporting all the way. **"**

JOE HART

England's No.1 in 2014 on the Three Lions at the 2018 World Cup

"I'm not particularly into people giving me credit. It's not something I think about. It's not important to me. The only thing that's important is if I'm doing my job properly on the pitch for the team and for the manager.**"**

JORDAN HENDERSON

no fan of faint praise

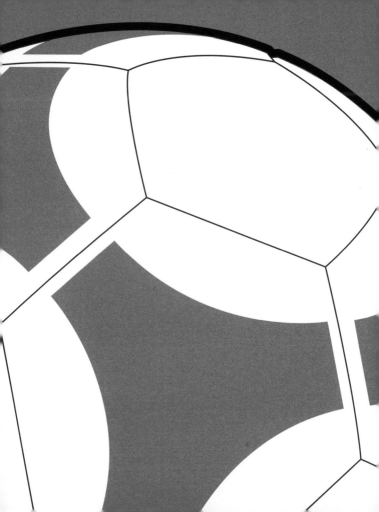

CHAPTER 3

THE TOUGHEST JOB IN FOOTBALL

❝The nicest thing about the England captaincy is that the manager gets the blame if things go wrong.**❞**

GARY LINEKER

England's leading scorer in World Cup finals

❝You have to accept that failure isn't impossible. In football we're branded either as winners or losers, but I think you are a failure only when you start to blame someone else for your failings.**❞**

ROY HODGSON

England manager between 2012 and 2016

❝To be really happy we must throw our hearts over the bar and hope our bodies will follow.**❞**

GRAHAM TAYLOR

reveals his tactical philosophy

"To be England manager you must win every game, not do anything in your private life and hopefully not earn too much money.**"**

SVEN-GORAN ERIKSSON

who earned millions as England coach

❝I said right at the start that I would live and die by results and results haven't gone my way. In that sense we have failed.**❞**

STEVE McCLAREN

who failed to lead the Three Lions to Euro 2008

❝They are not your players,
they are loaned from the club. You
just wheel them out for a game
for England.**❞**

KEVIN KEEGAN

on the eternal club versus country debate

The England job is an impossible job. Particularly for an Englishman, it's tougher than being Prime Minister.

GLENN HODDLE

England's 1998 World Cup coach

"We didn't underestimate them. They were a lot better than we thought.**"**

SIR BOBBY ROBSON

after England beat Cameroon 3-2 in the 1990 World Cup quarter-final

❝If history repeats itself, I should think we can expect the same thing again.**❞**

TERRY VENABLES

states the obvious

❝We're a team, with our diversity and our youth, that represents modern England. In England, we have spent a bit of time being a bit lost as to what our modern identity is. I think we represent that modern identity and hopefully, people can connect with us.**❞**

GARETH SOUTHGATE

reinvents the Three Lions

❝I'd walk over burning coals to get the England job. It's not an impossible job, because people keep doing it.**❞**

SAM ALLARDYCE

whose international managerial reign lasted one match

❝It's like a toaster, the referee's shirt pocket. Every time there's a tackle, up pops a yellow card.**❞**

KEVIN KEEGAN *on international officials*

"Any Englishman that is worth his salt would want to manage the England team.**"**

DON REVIE

England boss between 1974 and 1977

"The referee has just got me the sack. Thank him ever so much for that, won't you?"

GRAHAM TAYLOR

after England lost to the Netherlands in a World Cup qualifier in 1993

It's impossible to please everybody all of the time but you just have to believe that you're making decisions for the right reasons.

GARETH SOUTHGATE

refreshingly honest about the England coach's job

**❝People want success.
It's like coffee, they want instant.❞**

SIR BOBBY ROBSON

sums up the job succinctly

❝I can't stand the crap that gets talked by everyone – players, fans, the media, club officials. Why should I waste my time listening to people who are clearly less intelligent than me?❞

FABIO CAPELLO

England manager between 2008 and 2012, feels the pressure

❝If you can't stand the heat in the dressing room, get out of the kitchen.**❞**

TERRY VENABLES

mixes his metaphors

" For some it's the ultimate job.
For others, it's the last job. **"**

KEVIN KEEGAN

who coached two clubs before the England job ... and two after

" Being an ex-England manager, one that failed to qualify for the World Cup, is like being a dead politician. **"**

GRAHAM TAYLOR

who – eventually – was forgiven for missing out on USA 94

"If you are a fantastic painter, you are never rich until you are dead. And I think it's the same with managers. You're never appreciated until you're gone.**"**

SIR BOBBY ROBSON

tells it as it is

ffYou've beaten them once.
Now go out and bloody beat
them again. **jj**

SIR ALF RAMSEY

sends England out for extra-time in the 1966 World Cup final

" Being given chances and not taking them. That's what life is all about. **"**

RON GREENWOOD

took the Three Lions to Euro 1980 and the 1982 World Cup

"Football's always easier
when you've got the ball.**"**

KEVIN KEEGAN

England's coach at Euro 2000

CHAPTER 4

WORLD CUP HEROICS

"I was proud playing for England
in the World Cup. Every game I played in,
I did really, really well. I had the world at
my feet, you know.**"**

PAUL GASCOIGNE

England's standout player at Italia 90

❝The 1966 World Cup wasn't
won on the playing fields of England.
It was won on the streets.**❞**

SIR BOBBY CHARLTON
1966 World Cup winner

"When the final whistle went I was in shock. The next thing I knew I was on the floor with Nobby Stiles giving me a big, toothless kiss."

GEORGE COHEN

one of England's 11 heroes in the 1966 World Cup final

" We've made several pieces of history. Biggest win in the tournament. First knockout win for 10 years. First quarter-final win for longer. First win on penalties in the World Cup. We keep looking to break the barriers down. **"**

GARETH SOUTHGATE

on the Three Lions' 2018 World Cup journey

❝I think everyone around the world knows the tools are there in England's armoury to do well in a World Cup. The challenge is to go out there and prove it.**❞**

STEVEN GERRARD

captain of the Three Lions at the 2010 and 2014 World Cups

" Playing in a World Cup semi-final completely changes your life. There is a before and after playing in a game like that and, especially if you aren't one of the big stars, nothing is ever the same again. It makes an imprint in your life which never goes. **"**

PAUL PARKER

reflects on England's famous 1990 showdown with West Germany

"That save from Pele's header was the best I ever made. I didn't have any idea how famous it would become. To start with, I didn't even realise I'd made it at all.**"**

GORDON BANKS

on his iconic 1970 stop against Brazil

"In every World Cup there's always a player who comes from nowhere before every tournament, normally someone who gets in that you don't expect, and that happens all the time with England. **"**

GLENN HODDLE

in his case – France 1998 – it was 18-year-old Michael Owen

" There's nothing quite like a World Cup.
I would have been 10 years old and
I remember the World Cup coming up
and the usual hype around it. It was only
when the games started that I realised
what international football was all about.
I just loved it. **"**

MICHAEL OWEN

recalls the 1990 World Cup

"We are privileged to be out
here representing our country. The chance
to connect everyone through football and
make a difference to how people feel …
and they'll be inspiring youngsters.
That's more powerful than what we're
doing with our results.**"**

GARETH SOUTHGATE

after England reached the 2018 World Cup semi-finals

❝Along with 21 other guys who played in 1966 and went through all the emotions, I can tell them categorically that representing your country is the best feeling in football by a country mile.**❞**

SIR GEOFF HURST

the only man to score a World Cup final hat-trick

" The World Cup is a once in a lifetime opportunity – just give it your best. You're playing for your country in a World Cup, it can't get any better than that as a player, can it? **"**

ALAN SHEARER

England captain at the 1998 finals in France

97

"Nobody wants to be associated
with failing to qualify for the World Cup
finals. I cannot imagine the shame of it.**"**

RIO FERDINAND

who appeared in three World Cups

❝That goal in the 1998 World Cup
changed me – not as a person, but
as a player. People have looked at me
differently ever since. It gave me confidence
and now I feel I can achieve anything.**❞**

DAVID BECKHAM

on his free-kick against Colombia

❝I have dreamt of going to a
World Cup since I was a kid. Today
that dream came true. It's an honour to
represent the Three Lions this summer.**❞**

TRENT ALEXANDER-ARNOLD,

Liverpool defender on his selection for the 2018 World Cup

"You've got to believe you're going to win, and I believe we'll win the World Cup until the final whistle blows and we're knocked out. **"**

PETER SHILTON

who came close at Italia 90

"Whether you're male or female, going to a World Cup is the biggest thing that will ever happen in your life.**"**

PHIL NEVILLE

who wasn't in a finals squad but coached
England at the 2019 Women's World Cup

&& Bobby Moore was a national hero. The 1966 squad are all legends and that's what we would emulate. If we did, the West Ham fans might even forgive me everything. Maybe they'd claim me back as one of their own. **"**

FRANK LAMPARD

a former Hammer, ahead of the 2010 tournament

"We believe we can beat them. We are going to be underdogs, but that's the way we like it.**"**

PAUL INCE

ahead of England's round of 16 clash with Argentina in 1998

"It was my proudest moment as a manager when England drew 0–0 with Italy in Rome to qualify for the World Cup finals.**"**

GLENN HODDLE

leads the Three Lions to the 1998 tournament

❝People question whether the players care as much about international football these days, but playing in the World Cup is the dream. You're very aware that you're lucky to be there and also that you might not get another crack at it. A lot of nerves come with that.**❞**

DARREN ANDERTON

a member of England's 1998 World Cup campaign

❝It's impossible not to dream about lifting the World Cup, it's the biggest competition in the world. It's impossible not to think about that. Those dreams of lifting it, I'm sure we've all had them.**❞**

HARRY KANE

who captained England to the 2018 World Cup semi-final

❝ Coming out of the dressing room all we could hear was a beehive-like noise at the end of the tunnel. When we hit the open air the noise, movement and colour blew everything out of your mind. **❞**

GEORGE COHEN

1966 World Cup winner

" For me to get into the World Cup squad was the highlight of my career. I thoroughly enjoyed it. It's been an incredible month for me, I'm not sure it's sunk in yet, but I am sure when I get home I'll start to reflect on it all. **"**

FABIAN DELPH

on the 2018 finals

❝It was the most glorious moment of my life and England's greatest sporting achievement. It's been a privilege to look back at such an amazing time. The 1966 World Cup was a unique moment for this country and for me personally.**❞**

SIR BOBBY CHARLTON

reflects on England's glory at Wembley

"It is no good starting off like a sprinter if you soon run out of juice. To win a World Cup you have to build up momentum.**"**

TERRY BUTCHER

veteran of the 1982, 1986 and 1990 World Cup campaigns

CHAPTER 5

BEST OF ENEMIES

"It seemed a pity so much Argentinian talent is wasted. Our best football will come against the right type of opposition – a team who come to play football and not act as animals.**"**

SIR ALF RAMSEY

on England's 1–0 defeat of Argentina in
an ill-tempered 1966 World Cup quarter-final

" Why are the English the only people in the world who still claim the ball crossed the line in the 1966 World Cup final? **"**

BILD

German newspaper, still bitter about Sir Geoff Hurst's famous goal

"He said it was the 'Hand of God'. I said it was the hand of a rascal and I'm right. He was the best player in the world and he had the chance to be the best sportsman in the world too.**"**

SIR BOBBY ROBSON

on Diego Maradona's handball in the
1986 World Cup quarter-final in Mexico

❝They were probably the dirtiest team I've ever come up against, surrounding the referee, pushing the referee, the head-butt. I'd never seen a game like that before and how they behaved.**❞**

JOHN STONES

England defender unimpressed by Colombia
in the 2018 World Cup round of 16

❝What I saw of the English against the USA had very little to do with football. It looked to me as if the English have gone backwards into the bad old days of kick and rush.❞

FRANZ BECKENBAUER

the German legend puts the boot in at the 2010 World Cup

❝There was an in-built desire to beat Scotland when I was growing up and dreaming about getting into the England squad. The atmosphere when we played the Scots was always a little bit different, a bit louder. **❞**

GLENN HODDLE

on the oldest rivalry in world football

119

If Paul Gascoigne said anything to me after the game, I would have punched him.

ANDY GORAM

Scotland goalkeeper after England's Euro 96 victory at Wembley

66 I've never liked English football,
even if there are some great players
there. I don't like England either
because the weather is gloomy. **99**

FRANCESCO TOTTI

Italy and Roma striker

❝As we came around the corner from the 18th green, a crowd of members were at the clubhouse window waiting to tell me England had won the World Cup. It was the blackest day of my life.**❞**

DENIS LAW

Scotland legend unhappy with the Three Lions' 1966 triumph

❝We owe the English big time.
They stole our land, our oil, perpetrated
the Highland Clearances and now
they've even pinched Billy Connolly.**❞**

GORDON STRACHAN *1–0*
former Scotland player and manager

" There was a bit of pushing and a lot of banter. 'Wait until you come to Turkey,' was the shout, with fingers being passed across throats. And that was just the kit man. **"**

GARETH SOUTHGATE

remembers an ugly Euro 2004 qualifier against Turkey

❝I have no doubts whatsoever that Germany will thrash England. What could possibly go wrong? The English haven't beaten us in Munich for a hundred years.**❞**

ULI HOENESS

ex-German international, before England's 5–1 rout of Germany in 2001

"Football is a simple game. Twenty-two men chase a ball for 90 minutes and at the end, the Germans always win.**"**

GARY LINEKER

on being on the wrong end of the England v Germany rivalry

" That's how it is with the English. If you score against them, you're a good player. If you don't, you're not. **"**

ZLATAN IBRAHIMOVIC

After scoring all four of Sweden's goals in a 4-2 victory over England in 2012

ff [Joe] Hart looked very confident with himself, so I thought we had to bring him down a peg or two. **JJ**

ANDREA PIRLO

of Italy after his 'Panenka' penalty in the EURO 2012 quarter-final

"We know the English really don't bother about us. They have this sense of superiority that comes with thinking how much better they are than us. And that's why we go into a game like this, absolutely bursting to prove a point.**"**

SCOTT BROWN

Scotland midfielder, before a 2018 World Cup qualifier

"If you want to have a great party at Wembley, don't invite the Germans.**"**

ALAN SHEARER

after England lost their EURO 96 semi-final penalty shoot-out to them

" We have always favoured Welsh people because arguably the passion is there. Welsh most definitely, foreign possibly, but definitely not English. **"**

JONATHAN FORD

Welsh FA chief executive on the next Wales manager in 2017

❝Winning that game against England was enough. Winning the World Cup that year was secondary for us. Beating England was our real aim. To play against England is not to play against any team.**❞**

ROBERTO PERFUMO

*Argentina defender, on the losing side in 1966, on the
significance of their controversial 1986 World Cup quarter-final*

❝For me what mattered was that we had lost to the Jocks and I have never gone home from Wembley in such a bad mood. I was furious.**❞**

STUART PEARCE

on England's 1–0 loss to Scotland in 1999, even though they qualified for Euro 2000, 2–1 on aggregate

66My dream is to play England
in the final – and beat them without
even the need for extra time.**99**

MESUT ÖZIL

Germany's England-based midfielder
looks ahead to the 2018 World Cup

“We proved everything differently that people were talking. Especially English journalists, pundits from television, they underestimated Croatia tonight and that was a huge mistake. As I said, they should be more humble and respect opponents more.**”**

LUKA MODRIC

Croatia midfielder, after their 2018 World Cup semi-final win

" When England play Scotland at anything, even if it's tiddlywinks, they want to win. That's the way it is and always has been. **"**

MARK HATELEY

former England striker

"Jocks love to beat England. Forget the World Cup, European finals, for Scottish fans, beating England is everything. It's a history thing, simple as that. Go back centuries, to the battles of Bannockburn, Falkirk or Culloden; at the end of the day the Scots like beating the English.**"**

ALAN HANSEN

former Scotland international

" Boy, I feel sorry for these bastards. How are they ever going to live down the fact we beat them? **"**

HARRY KEOUGH

US defender, after the shock 1–0 World Cup
win over England in 1950

" Maybe this wasn't the greatest Scotland team ever to tread the Wembley turf. But it was certainly great enough to make chumps out of the World Cup champs. **"**

THE SUNDAY POST

gloats as Scotland beat world champions England 3–2 in April 1967

CHAPTER 6

CELEBRITY FANS

❝I think for many people my age, the best moment as an England fan was Italia 90. I'm pretty sure that's when I fell in love with football. David Platt and Paul Gascoigne were my heroes that summer.**❞**

JAMES CORDEN

British comedian and host of US television's The Late, Late Show

CELEBRITY FANS

" When I first met him, I didn't know whether to shake his hand or lick his face. **"**

ROBBIE WILLIAMS
singer, on David Beckham

143

❝Your real ability as a sportsman and as a person shines through when life gets hard and you're out of nick, the team is faltering and the public is no longer on your side. It is those situations for which David Beckham was born.**❞**

SIR IAN BOTHAM

cricket legend, who played a few
Football League games for Scunthorpe

66Thanks to the England team
and manager for giving us this beautiful
World Cup run. It's been a ride.**99**

DAVID BADDIEL

comedian and singer of 'Three Lions', after the 2018 World Cup

❝The 2014 World Cup is an amazing moment for the nation to come together. It is truly a global festival of football where great names take their chance to shine. I am proud to be associated with the England team and really look forward to seeing what happens in Brazil.**❞**

PRINCE WILLIAM

Duke of Cambridge

❝I'm proud to be an England fan and enjoy nothing more than joining in with the crowd to get behind the team. I'm as passionate about the England team as the next man.**❞**

RAY WINSTONE

actor and the FA's 2006 World Cup
ambassador for good behaviour

It is rare a man can be that tough on the field and also have his own line of underwear.

BARACK OBAMA

former President of the United States, on David Beckham

"We're all fans of England. My eldest lad was distraught in the pub when they went out in the semi-finals and he was crying, like properly crying.**"**

NOEL GALLAGHER

former Oasis songwriter, on the Three Lions' 2018 World Cup exit

❝I think my earliest memory was the 1998 World Cup. I watched England beat Colombia in a church hall and then remember seeing David Beckham getting sent off against Argentina. I watched that one at home and was gutted. The first reaction was, 'what have you done?'**❞**

ALISTAIR BROWNLEE

double Olympic triathlon champion

My favourite player by a mile is Gazza. He was by far the best dribbler ever. A lot of rubbish is written about George Best and Maradona – the best ever is Gazza.

TIM VINE

comedian, on England's star at Italia 90

❝You did us proud. Real grit, determination and never giving up until the very end. You should hold your heads up high.**❞**

LEWIS HAMILTON

six-time Formula One champion, on England's 2018 World Cup campaign

" The team over-achieved, played some really decent football and totally reset the nation's attitude to international football. What a great summer they gave us. **"**

JACK WHITEHALL

comedian, reflects on the 2018 World Cup

❝I spoke to the O2 and for the first time ever doors will open at 6:30pm and we're going to play England versus Croatia up on my big screens, so come here and we'll watch it together. We're going to watch this together, and you know what? It's coming home.**❞**

JUSTIN TIMBERLAKE

American singer whose concert clashed with the 2018 World Cup semi-final

" I'm just about old enough to remember England winning in 1966. I think for any English football fan that has to be the greatest moment and I guess it was the third Geoff Hurst goal that really was the greatest moment of them all. **"**

LORD COE

former Olympic champion and head of the London 2012 Olympic Games

❝However you break it down, England have had a fantastic 2018 World Cup and we should all be very proud of our boys. **❞**

CARL FROCH

former super middleweight boxing world champion

❝It's brilliant to be the first band ever to launch an England shirt. When Umbro approached us, we jumped at the chance and loved the idea of revealing the away shirt in one of our great footballing rivals' country. When the World Cup is on, it's all about England. **❞**

TOM MEIGHAN

Kasabian front man who wore England's new kit at a concert in Paris in 2010

"I've dreamed about playing for England in a World Cup-winning team, beating Brazil. As an England fan, you have to believe we are going to win.**"**

ED BALLS

former Labour Party politician

"TS Eliot may well have measured his life out in coffee spoons, but I measure mine in England's World Cups.**"**

RUSSELL BRAND

comedian, writing in The Guardian, *in June 2018*

"An English World Cup campaign
will almost certainly include a meltdown,
and there will be panic, and introspection,
and calls for something, anything, to be
done to – or by, or for – somebody. But
it's going to be all right in the end.**"**

NICK HORNBY

author of Fever Pitch *and* High Fidelity

"The greatest thing about supporting England is that it gives supporters of smaller clubs a taste of the big time.**"**

TIM LOVEJOY

broadcaster and former presenter of Sky Sports' Soccer AM

❝Only four more years until England qualify for the World Cup. Yay! Come on England!**❞**

RICKY GERVAIS

*comedian, after the Three Lions were
knocked out of the 2014 World Cup*

"We were going through the last rapids out of the Andes. Our guide was trying to get the radio to work. Suddenly he shouted 'I've got it!' We got the last few minutes and penalty shoot-out. We couldn't believe we were listening to the Wembley roar from so far away.**"**

MICHAEL PALIN

Monty Python member and adventurer, recalls
the England v Spain EURO 96 quarter-final

"Sad. Proud. Annoyed.
Relieved. Disappointed. Unsurprised.
Impressed. Vexed. Gutted. Elated.
Deflated. Despondent. Encouraged.
Defeated. Defiant. Broken. Resilient.
Inspired. Silly. All those things.**"**

STEPHEN FRY

presenter, author and actor on England's 2018 World Cup elimination

❝You know what? Football did come home – brought us together, made us proud, gave us something to cheer.**❞**

NICK ROBINSON

journalist and BBC presenter, on the
Three Lions' 2018 World Cup exploits

CHAPTER 7

THE WEMBLEY ROAR

"I went to see England against Switzerland at Wembley with my dad and brother. That was in 2008. It was Fabio Capello's first game in charge. Jermaine Jenas scored and we won 2–1. I remember the national anthem was incredible. I sang it with pride – always do.**"**

HARRY KANE

England's captain at the World Cup in Russia

"Wembley is the cathedral of football. It is the capital of football and it is the heart of football.**"**

PELÉ

Brazil legend, who never actually played at Wembley

❝Wembley is almost sacred
territory when it comes to English football.
All of us who love the game have
special memories of the place.**❞**

GLENN HODDLE

who played and managed England at the Home of Football

"When I was a kid seeing English football played at Wembley in all competitions, important games, the tradition there with the two managers going out, I loved that.**"**

PEP GUARDIOLA

former Spain midfielder and Manchester City manager

"Wembley is special. Players always realise it is a big thing to play there, whether it's in a Cup final or representing your country. When we played there, the crowd was usually 100,000 and the fans made a tremendous amount of noise.**"**

GORDON BANKS

1966 World Cup winner

❝Whether you are white, brown, purple or blue, it's the same. When you are fortunate enough to make your debut for England at Wembley, it's the greatest feeling in the world.**❞**

VIV ANDERSON

who made his debut against Czechoslovakia at Wembley in November 1978

❝If you ask me, I am so happy to play at Wembley. When you love football, always you hear about Wembley. When I played in the old Wembley in 2000, it was a dream come true. Every game I play at Wembley is a gift.**❞**

MAURICIO POCHETTINO

former Argentina defender and Tottenham Hotspur manager

❝It is as an awesome, magnificent, inspiring venue. Walking out across the pitch from the dressing rooms gives you goose bumps. **❞**

JAMIE REDKNAPP

*former England midfielder whose caps
were won at the old stadium*

"At Wembley, everything is bigger, wider. The atmosphere is different.**"**

LOTHAR MATTHÄUS

German legend who played in two Wembley friendlies

"I played for England at cricket and football. Playing at Wembley in front of 60,000 people seemed better than playing at Cirencester in front of my family and friends.**"**

PHIL NEVILLE

who played at the old and new Wembley stadiums

❝To go out at Wembley and score is what you dream about as a kid.**❞**

HARRY KANE

who has done it quite a lot for club and country

"Long before I was a player, I recall walking down Wembley Way to watch England schoolboys play Germany schoolboys in 1970 and the excitement and anticipation of finally seeing the famous old stadium. I was only 12 and a trip to Wembley was a huge day out.**"**

GLENN HODDLE

who graced the stadium on numerous occasions

"Wembley has got a tremendous image around the world. Everybody has heard of it."

JESUS NAVAS

Spain winger, an unused substitute in an
October 2011 friendly under the Arch

❝When you reach Wembley, you think of the amount of hours you have put in training throughout your life, all the games you have played up to that point... it is there forever as a reward. **❞**

JAMES MILNER

veteran of 61 England internationals across eight seasons

❝ Wembley is the greatest football
stadium in the world, with all the history
that goes with that place. **❞**

PAOLO DI CANIO

much-travelled Italian striker, who never actually played at Wembley

"The Olympic Stadium in Munich and Maracana in Rio are also stadiums which as a professional player you want to play in, but for me Wembley was special. I had always been fascinated by the place. It has always been my dream to run out on its turf.**"**

OSSIE ARDILES

Argentinean World Cup winner, who played in England for more than 10 years

"It is an unbelievable feeling to score for England at Wembley."

JAMIE VARDY

who had that 'unbelievable feeling' four times

"Wembley is a ground with great history. It's hosted games and players of great prestige. It's always important playing on great stages like this.**"**

DIEGO COSTA

Spain striker who played at Wembley but only in club football

❝Leading a team out at Wembley is a big thing and it is a special occasion. It is always a massive incentive and motivation for any player.**❞**

STEVEN GERRARD

who captained England 38 times in 114 internationals

❝At Wembley it got warmer and warmer as you went up the tunnel and what hit you, apart from the noise, was the smell of fried onions.❞

MALCOLM MACDONALD

England striker from the 1970s who recalled the atmosphere of the old stadium

❝Leading out the England team, it felt like Wembley was my ground, the night, everything, belonged to me.**❞**

DAVID PLATT

on captaining England for the first time in 1990

❝I grew up five minutes from the stadium and watched it being built. I'd play football right outside and look up at this huge stadium with all the cranes and building work and think, 'One day, when it's finished, I need to be playing in here'.**❞**

RAHEEM STERLING

named Man of the Match in his first game at Wembley against Denmark in 2014

"I've been fortunate enough to play in
some great stadiums but we all know
Wembley's history. I used to look at it and
say 'one day, hopefully, if I'm lucky enough, I
could be playing there'. I've had a love affair
with this place since I was a kid.**"**

PETER CROUCH

*England's tallest goalscorer, the 6ft 7in
striker scored 22 times in 44 games*

❝For the players, it's a special stadium to play at, one of the grounds you dream of playing at as a youngster.**❞**

KEVIN DE BRUYNE

Belgium midfielder who has yet to play an international at Wembley

ff Three lions on a shirt
Jules Rimet still gleaming
Thirty years of hurt
Never stopped me dreaming. **""**

DAVID BADDIEL AND FRANK SKINNER

*lyrics from the song, written with the Lightning Seeds, when England
hosted EURO 96*